Passive Personalities

Is it passive aggressive personality?

Difficult?

Stubborn?

Hostile?

Free Yourself NOW!

2nd edition

by Margaret Brown

Table of Contents

Introduction

There are going to be times in your life when you feel out of control of a situation and this may or may not be as a result of passive aggression. However, can you recognize it when it happens to you? Do you know what passive aggression is or how it can affect you? Are you behaving in a passive aggressive way to others?

Your relationships, if strained, may incorporate an element of passive aggressive behavior on the part of someone. You may not know it because this kind of behavior hides behind a façade and doesn't always make itself clear. It's every bit as harmful as aggression, which is shown in a physical way and can indeed have long term effects mentally. The damage done by people who use passive aggressiveness can be long lasting. It can indeed last longer than the bruises left after a beating. Children who experience it may continue right through their adulthood to feel the effects.

If you want to understand this kind of behavior and want to be able to recognize it and do something about it, then this book gives you a golden opportunity to do just that. The very first step is understanding, and if you're not sure what it is or how it affects you and your relationships with others, it's time you did understand it. This book explains all about relationships and the way that people manipulate each other in different ways. Within the realms of that manipulation passive aggressiveness lurks. When it hits you between the eyes, it hurts. When you use it to hurt others, it has a lasting impact, but not a positive one.

Psychologists have their work cut out for them because those who suffer from passive aggressive behavior or as a result of it may find themselves talking to professionals in order to find answers. However, if you are interested in human relationships and want to make the best of those that you have, learning about it in advance of it happening will help you to understand and to either stem your own use of it or to stop others' aggressiveness hurting you.

Chapter 1 – What is Passive Aggressiveness?

When you make someone feel small or in fact make him or her feel a certain amount of lack of trust toward you, you may just be using passive aggression. It's sometimes hard to recognize in your own actions. In fact, if you were described by that same person as being passive aggressive, you would quite probably think that it was a little bit of an exaggeration. However, passive aggressive people can do more harm to others than they may anticipate. If you've ever had someone who is nice to you, but then who talks about you in a negative way behind your back, you may also have experienced passive aggressive behavior. When something that is spoken goes against what is actually meant, this is where passive aggression finds its starting point. It's a form of sarcasm but it's much more harmful to those who experience it. It takes away trust and leaves the recipient wondering what just happened.

Aggression in its violent and physical form is actually easier to understand. There is no misconstrued message to a punch on the nose. However, when little digs are made at you that make you feel irritated to the point of anger, it amounts to the same thing. It's just a more subtle way of punching you in the nose without using a fist. Some people are very gifted at using passive aggressiveness and may cause problems for others by practicing it. Do you have anyone who purposely tries to wind you up? If they succeed, they have used passive aggression to do that. Thus, you can see passive aggression as being anger or aggression that one feels as a result of something that someone else has done.

Why people use passive aggressive behavior

There are many who are frustrated themselves in that they want to express anger, but know it's inappropriate. In the example shown below, you will see exactly what this means. Jenny's mom wants Jenny to clean her room. Jenny doesn't want to do it.

Mom: Can you please clean your room Jenny? We have relatives coming and it's a real mess."

Jenny: In a minute mom. I will do it in a minute.

Mom (an hour later): You haven't started on your room yet.

Jenny actually feels angry with her mom for interfering with her time. She has more important things to do. However, she knows that she can't just tell her mom to go away or be rude to her, although she would dearly love to be at this moment in time. Instead, she uses passive aggressive behavior to pass that anger in her mom's direction.

Jenny: It's okay mom, I will do it.

Mom (another hour later) arrives with the vacuum cleaner and starts to clean the room. She is angry. She is slamming things around and she takes out her feeling of anger on her daughter. Although Jenny didn't intentionally make mom angry, the anger gives her a sense of being on the winning side so achieves her aims.

People such as Jenny who have communication problems and are unable to express their feelings in a more appropriate way, are very likely to use passive aggressive behavior to counteract their lack of social ability. The reactions of someone who is passive aggressive, are often fueled by negative and quite possibly inappropriate feelings about being asked to do something. Typical responses in this case may be:

- Mom is always picking on me.
- Mom keeps interfering in my life.
- Nothing I do is good enough for mom.
- Mom is unreasonable

The problem is that the reaction that they get confirms what they believe so they get to feel in control and full understanding of situations when, in fact, they are far from in control.

Thus, you can see that passive aggression is misplaced anger, manifested by passing the anger on to someone else. It is unresolved anger until a reaction is achieved. When someone else loses his or her temper because of the passive aggressive behavior, the perpetrator has achieved the objective and feels very smug and self-satisfied. In this case, Jenny's mom behaved like she was unreasonable by slamming around her daughter's room in a way that isn't very adult and in doing so confirmed Jenny's belief that mom is always picking on her and keep interfering in her life. This behavior, which is almost paramount to a tantrum by her mother, also confirms in Jenny's mind that her mother is unreasonable. Thus, Jenny feels empowered.

Chapter 2 – Who Displays This Behavior?

The people that display this kind of behavior are usually those who cannot express themselves very well. They may use comments intended to irritate. They may use tactics that they know will upset someone else, but they are also the least likely to admit that they have a problem. Why? These are people who act out their anger and repressed thoughts through others. They don't shout; they don't seem to make unreasonable claims of other people and see themselves as reasonable. The problem is that they can be exceptionally manipulative of situations and of individuals.

A man, for example, who doesn't know how to help his wife with her problems, may try passive aggressiveness to make her feel that her problems are irrational. That way, he passes the buck back to her. His lack of answers and his seeming disinterest in her problems may reduce her to tears of frustration and anger, but then he is able to justify his actions by saying that it's very hard to help someone who is so emotional. You have to see the full circle to understand who displays this behavior and you may even do it yourself without being aware of it. If you were, then the better course would be to be more honest and less devious in your dealings with others. If it becomes a regular habit, you will begin to use it to avoid having to face responsibilities or to pass blame and it's far better that you start to look at life from another person's perspective.

Let's try and demonstrate so that you understand the kind of person who would use this kind of behavior. Supposing that you live in a house with fellow students. One of them isn't pulling her weight and doesn't bother to clean the bathroom after having used it. There are always traces of soggy soap, rings around the bathtub and generally the room is left in a mess. There are several ways that people could deal with a problem such as this.

The aggressive stance – This would make you likely to shout at her. Intimidation and threats are frequent if you are an aggressive person. You see the answers lying in making someone afraid of consequences.

The passive stance – The passive personality does things another way. They "pass" the responsibility of managing a situation to someone else. These are the ostriches that bury their heads in the sand in the hope that things will change all on their own.

The assertive stance – In this case, an assertive person would take the view that discussing the problem and bringing it to the knowledge of the offender is the only way forward. This helps them to understand what exactly is being done in a wrongful manner.

So where does the passive aggressive attitude come into the picture?

Since a passive person would do nothing and an aggressive person would be inclined to beat sense into someone, where's the line that people cross in order to become passive aggressive? Psychologists believe that the passive aggressive person develops their habits within the years of childhood. These may be people whose parents controlled everything or who led the child to believe that the child's opinion was of little value. That child grows up with that belief firmly entrenched in their way of thinking and thus will keep quiet when opinions are required. However, they may also feel very repressed by not being able to express opinion and may use this to passively be the cause of anger in others. Why would they want to do this? If vilifies them to see that their actions actually caused anger and justifies the action because they then no longer have to feel repressed. The person who displayed the anger took the bait. They lay that bait, very passively as that's the way they do things, but the result was aggression and that was what they were aiming at. People like this need reactions. They need someone to get angry or upset because it helps them to vilify what they feel. That's important to them. If that inner feeling can't be expressed in any way, then it merely serves to make the individual continue to think that they have everything wrong, as their parents would have made him/her believe as a child.

Passive aggressiveness used to be considered as a mental illness or ailment that had its own special slot in the psychiatric world. However, since most people do, at some stage within their lives, display passive aggressiveness, it was taken from the registry of mental illnesses and treated as part and parcel of personality itself.

You should always look out for certain patterns of behavior with passive aggressive people. Are they the sort to agree to do something and then make things so difficult for you that you are forced to take back the task you asked them to do? In the workplace, at home and within your groups of friends, be sure there are people who will use passive aggressiveness to let you down or to cause you inconvenience and disappointment.

These people are those who give all the right answers, but then who avoid all responsibility when it comes to getting things done. Instead, they are much more likely to stir up antagonism and anger in others because they don't know how else to respond to a situation which causes them discomfort or inconvenience.

If you were to look through your friends and family, you would find people who make all kinds of promises and then let people down. You would find people who say all the right things and then shock you by turning everyone against you. The danger of this kind of person is that the potential that they have to cause emotional disruption and anger to kick in among those who have to deal with them on a regular basis. Avoiding those kinds of people is obviously the best bet, but what if you are one of them? Examine your motives for disappointing people and learn to say "no" instead of giving false hopes.

The way that this works is that you don't leave people hanging onto your word that you will get something done when you have no intention of doing it. Thus, if you can learn to let your true voice be heard, there's no need to disappoint anyone and you can walk away from the task having been honest in your communication with others. That's a far more constructive solution.

Chapter 3: How to Stem Passive Aggressive Behavior

In your life, you come across a lot of people. There will be those who, through the example they have set to you, you can trust. These are people who are reliable. They don't make mistakes. They don't get involved in arguments and they are friendly and positive. You will also come across people who leech from others. They don't have sufficient character to be givers. These are the toxic people who demand of you all the time or who, trusted with something you have asked of them, will let you down.

Make a note of people who cause negativity in your life and see if you can avoid these people as much as possible. If they make you angry, analyze why. If you are unable to tackle the substance of your discontent by talking to these people, then it's likely that these are people best put out of your life.

The way to avoid passive aggressive behavior is to recognize its potential. If something that someone says to you upsets you in any way, learn from taking a step back rather than reacting. They may be trying to stir up a situation and may not actually have the balls to do it themselves. If this is the case, confrontation is hardly likely to get results. A quiet word in their ear may help you to stop them from behaving in this way with you. If they don't get the reaction that they want, they will use their tactics on someone else.

If you find yourself acting in a manner that is likely to upset someone else, ask yourself why. The difficulty is that you need to know what it is within you that make you react in that way. What is it that you want a response to?

If you go back through your childhood years, you will probably discover that you went through all kinds of experiences where your voice was never heard. Perhaps you had few friends at school. Perhaps your parents were too protective and didn't level with you about life and, as a consequence, you learned the hard way that life wasn't as simple as they led you to believe. You do need to face up to life and realize that you are being passive aggressive because it's harmful and can hurt people. Yes, you may get a kick from causing anger or causing an argument between others, but at the end of the day, you didn't get past the problem. You simply sidetracked your anger and aimed it at someone else whom you expected to react. That's a little unfair isn't it?

Supposing that you are passive aggressive. You are asked to do something that you really don't want to do. The chances are that you will do the job half-heartedly at best and actually let someone down at worst. So how should you avoid passive aggressive behavior that angers the person who trusted you with a given task?

- Tell them straight that you don't want to do it.
- Tell them that they have caught you at an inconvenient time.
- Tell them that you don't like doing it.

These are honest answers. It leaves someone in no doubt. If you are reasonable and give a friendly answer in the negative, they won't be expecting you to do the task. Saying that you are sorry and that it's not possible for you to do the job gives them no reason for anger unless they feel that you owe them and should remember that. Saying you will do it and then doing it in a half-hearted way isn't doing you any favors. If they get angry, you laugh to yourself about it because it's what you expect to happen, but think how much better you would feel in yourself had you learned to trust your own judgment a little better and communicated that you couldn't do the task in question.

Passive aggressive behavior and bullying

Watch a bully pick on someone. What he expects is submission. He expects the person he is picking on to be weaker. When he hurts someone, it gives him a great buzz because it makes him feel powerful. In the same way, the passive aggressive person bullies, but they do it in a covert manner. Avoid being the cause of discomfort and anger to anyone by learning to communicate. This is the answer to every problem in life and the overall happiness that it gives you is worth more than the smug reaction of passing anger to someone else.

If you have self-worth problems, look into them if they are affecting your relationship with other people. Talk to an expert or to an advisor. There may be much better ways of learning all the good things there are about you to help mend your self-esteem issues without having to resort to making people around you feel uncomfortable and ill at ease.

Chapter 4 - How to Recognize Passive Aggressive Behavior

Is there anyone in particular that always makes you mad and that seems to take pleasure in winding you up? There are probably a few people like that. The workplace is filled to brimming with different personalities and some react in different ways to the way you do. Imagine this scenario:

Coworker: It's unreasonable to expect us to work overtime this weekend.

You (Ken):   Yes it is. I had plans to go out with my girlfriend.

Coworker to Boss: You know you are ruining Ken's chances of ever getting laid.

You feel outraged because you told the coworker in confidence, just as he appeared to be confiding in you. He didn't give you any information that you could use as ammunition, but he's angry with the boss and instead of pointedly saying so, he uses you as the person who is angry. The boss then sees you as the problem. All too often, we leave ourselves open to being hurt, to being used by the passive aggressive personality because we tell them too much about ourselves. This kind of personality is the type who will announce your darkest secret to the whole office behind your back. This is the kind of person who will sympathize to your face and ridicule you when you are not there to defend yourself. The passive aggressive style is always covert.

Recognizing the style

Listen to people and observe. This tells you a lot about who they are. Is there a particular ringleader when problems occur? Remember, the passive aggressive person won't be that ringleader. They will be in the wings waiting to do damage. It may be someone overshadowed by a strong personality within the office environment. Since they were accustomed to having their opinions considered unimportant by their parents, they are not likely to proffer opinion. However, if they feel they can get an angry response from someone by stirring things up covertly, they will.

The problem with people like this is that they sit in the

background and wait for opportunity to come their way.

Boss: Is there anyone that wants to help out with the local school raffle.

Office wise guy: Count me out; I have too many commitments already.

Passive Aggressive guy: You could try Angela in accounts. She likes stuff like that.

The passive aggressive guy looks like he's taking part. He isn't. He knows that Angela in accounts is the least likely to want to help, but he's passing on the message that she might. Thus, he is building up the expectations of the boss for Angela to respond in a positive way. When she doesn't, he's likely to get offended. If he gets offended and voices his discontent, then the passive aggressive guy has actually won the day. No one will have noticed that it was him that caused the negativity except him. Angela's upset because she has too much on her plate already. She is everybody's doormat and when the boss approached the passive aggressive guy already knew how she felt because she was near to tears telling him that she's had enough.

Passive aggressiveness isn't nice. Its playing games with other people lives to gain power and if you find someone that needs to do that, they have problems of their own.

They don't know how to deal with communication. They don't know how to make their voice heard, so instead of doing that, the only way they feel they have any say at all is to mess things up for other people. You may have heard of the expression "mind games." These are the games played by people who have been told that they are useless. Those who don't know how to be effective play these. They are also played by people who have self-esteem issues and can only gain pleasure from seeing others put down or by transferring anger through the use of covert or underhanded behavior.

Observation

Your best tactic to avoid becoming the victim to someone who is exercising passive aggressiveness is to observe. Observe how people behave. Observe their honesty levels. Observe how they talk about people who are not in the room. It's important to recognize self-esteem issues. You can always offer someone in this situation a job you know that they can master and shower him or her with praises when they do it well. Perhaps, at the same time as stemming their necessity to use passive aggressive behavior, you may do something toward correcting problems left from childhood and help them to gain self-esteem.

Chapter 5 - Keys in Unlocking Yourself from the Passive Aggression Curse

When the fear of having this psychological problem starts to dawn on you, it is likely that you would develop a chain of stressors that will further bring you down. In addition, this might also push you to dabble in a series of unhealthy self-treatment and self-diagnosis. So before you harm yourself further, you need to do these first: STOP and BREATHE slowly.

The impulsive reaction to any situation with hostility would only trigger a mountain of issues to resolve later on. Furthermore, being unable to discern the difference between bullying and being passive progressive encourage you to plunge into extreme treatments later on. These are certainly NOT the solutions. But you can still help yourself in a healthier way or two by firstly educating yourself on the general characteristics of passive aggressiveness. Once you are able to see more clearly the triggering factors, then you can start scouring for real treatments that are suitable for you, for your needs, and for your overall health conditions.

But if you are genuinely concern about your health and behavior, then you may want to do the following right away:

KEY #01: Acknowledge that you have a problem!

Muster up the courage to tell yourself that ---yes, you may have a problem. It may not be easy to admit this at the beginning, but this will naturally lead you to the second key – to acknowledge that there are solutions, too. Do not be under the spell of constant denial, as it would not help you in any case. The problem is right there and that you have the power to say – you will need to address it the best way you can.

KEY #02: Re-evaluate your own habits

Habits are developed – they do not just appear overnight. Try to distinguish what sets you off. Be sensitive to the reaction of others, too. If you see any sign of them getting offended by what you just said, then maybe there could be something wrong with your choice of words and delivery. Take note of these, and use these notes when you reflect.

KEY #03: Do not embrace the idea of COMMUNICATING an instant and miracle cure

It is simply because it is not. The false impression that many people with behavioral issues, such as passive aggressiveness, is that they rely so much on idea that communicating with others would instantaneously address the problem. The issue with behavior takes more than just a mere 'girl talk' or 'man-to-man' talk. It requires a careful process of self-analysis, professional assistance, and reformulation of habits. In short, there is not such a thing as a 'quick-fix'.

KEY #04: Know your limits – get the professional help you need

In that, you want to clearly rid yourself of all the doubts, speculations, and fear of having this psychological disorder, you will have to be ready to exhaust all possible options when necessary. If you feel that it is just too much for you to handle on your own, you may want to start scouting for others' help. However, you will also have to be extra vigilant in getting the right help from the right individual. Therapists who are experts on cognitive-behavioral disorders are among the good options. Counseling is also sought by people who may have been suffering from psychological issues for a long time, but are not aware of it. There are also a number clinics focusing on behavioral disorders treatment that you may want to visit.

KEY #05: Focus on your strengths

So people are telling you off about your passive aggression, but that does not mean you will have to live with it your entire life. Instead of being overly pessimistic on what you have to deal with, try redirecting your thoughts to the things you are good at. Spend extra time with friends rather than voluntarily cordoning yourself off from the rest of the world. Break the social barriers you have been dealing with. Find an inspiring book to read. Rediscover your passions again. In short, make your brain work for/with you and not against you. Give yourself some time to dwell on happy thoughts. Meditate if you can. This will also allow you to create positive thoughts and habits.

These five keys can help you break free from the chains of Passive Aggression and its long-term psychological effects. They can only be used IF and WHEN you allow them to be part of your personal solutions.

Chapter 6: Eight Easy-to-Follow Tips in Addressing Passive Aggression

Saying good-bye to Passive Aggressive Behavior does not always require technical or complex treatment. By having the right attitude and approach to the disorder, you may still be able to break away from its chain. It is, like with all other things, and is a matter of choice. If you choose to be well, then you can start with the following tips:

Tip#01: Manage your stress level. Being in a stressful environment is a major triggering factor of such behavior. The mismanaged stress levels could branch into several behavioral issues. Breathing exercises, meditating, and exercises are among the suggested stress-busting activities.

Tip#02: Sweat it out. Exercising and doing physical activities have natural calming and soothing effect that do not only slash off stress but also pose improvement on your overall health. Sweating it out could also help you maintain a positive outlook in life, good mood, and better judgment skills.

Tip#03: When eating, choose healthily! You have heard this over and over again, but eating healthy is essential in kicking your metabolism up a gear. Starting your day with a healthy breakfast then moving with balanced meals for lunch and dinner can help you feel nourished right away. A nourished body keeps that brain healthy, too. This means you can instantly get rid of pessimism. The lack of pessimism and negative emotions means fewer chances of becoming passive aggressive.

Tip#04: Clear up your thoughts. When your brain is inundated with thoughts and worries, you naturally have better judgment in several matters. Take a few minutes during the day just to be quiet and not think of any work and family related matters. This quiet time can also quiet your body and mood.

Tip#05: Listen to what others tell you. The immediate reactions of the people around you can send you signals about your own behavior. Seeing a pattern in their reactions should remind you on how you normally react towards them. Be mindful and about these signals.

Tip#06: Sleep well. Yes, when you are tired from sleeping insufficient number of hours, you have the tendency to stuff yourself up to boost energy. Being sleepy may also encourage you to get food loaded with caffeine and release your tension with hostility. Make sure you get your 40 winks to avoid an extra 40 lbs.

Tip#07: Make it a habit to write what you during the day. An agenda is vital so you can keep track of what you have to finish in a day - the type of activity, as well as your will to do them, allow you to understand your habits. Do you procrastinate a lot? Are you easily distracted? The agenda may give you a clear idea on how severe your procrastination habits are.

Tip#08: Bust boredom away. Idling your time away can also be a contributor to being passive aggressive. Having nothing to do or being overly unproductive may lead to passive aggression. When you are bored, try engaging yourself in other hobbies like painting, sports, scrap booking, or gardening.

Chapter 7: Are You Passive-Aggressive?

Many people get the false impression that demonstrating passive aggression is tantamount to being a mean and bad person. Renowned psychotherapist and author Tina Gilbertson addressed this misconception and stated, "Being passive aggressive is considered a strategy as it is used by people who believe they do not have the right to be vocal about their feelings and that they tend to be afraid of being honest."

Most people who are passive-aggressive do not actually know that they have these behavioral issues. Most of the time, they also tend to feel bad about those people with the same issue. When people point it out to them at some point, these people tend to repel and deny. The problem is, most people feel offended when others demonstrate passive aggression. However, it is never easy to tell when we demonstrate the same behavior ourselves.

If you are worried that you may be showing passive aggression against others, then you may want to reflect on the following signs and ask yourself: Am I constantly doing these to my friends and colleagues? Do I easily offend the people around me? Am I afraid of being honest? To understand your behavior better, see the following list of behavior displayed by a passive aggressive person.

1. Have a tendency to make wistful and regretful statements

People that tend to be passive aggressive are those who are unable to ask for certain things directly regardless of how much they really desire these things. For example, when friends are invited to an event and you have not been invited but would really want to be in that event, you might say, " How I wish I could really go."

Another example of reaction from a passive aggressive person when he wants something so badly, but cannot afford to purchase it, " I wish I could buy those, but unfortunately, my salary is not even enough for my basic needs." Although these cases may seem simple, they are already signs for being passive aggressive. The best way to address this is to practice being direct. For example, you may say, " Could I go to the party, too?" or "May I just need to save more for those shoes." These statements would prevent other people from feeling guilty towards what you cannot have.

2. Being overly quiet

Silence is one of the most commonly used tools of the passive-aggressive people. This problem comes in different forms. At home, if you were told off due to something you did wrong and decided to use 'silent treatment' as a form of your protest, and then you can be considered a passive aggressive person. The same thing can be seen at work. If you are giving your colleagues the silent treatment or deliberately giving them the cold shoulder just because they made funny remarks about your work, then you have the sign of being passive aggressive.

If you are not capable of being 'all-ears' when in a meeting and prefer to use your mobile phone, chat, text, see what's on Facebook, or playing a game – then you have the classic sign of passive aggression. Moreover, such behavior may be easily perceived as rudeness. If you are worried that you may be passive aggressive unintentionally, then you start breaking certain habits and formulate new ones. For instance, try not to take your phone with you during a meeting, and give yourself a new task like jotting down notes for future reference.

Another form of passive aggression using silence is by deliberately ignoring calls and text messages from people. Pretending not to know them or being asleep despite the urgency of the calls is one of the most common ways passive aggressive people use. The problem with this is that you may be showing hints of problems, but are not ready to resolve these problems. Experts say that while you are showing aggression and even protests by doing these, you may also be punishing yourself, too.

3. Have the habit of keeping score

Sure, life is sometimes about taking a plunge into friendly competitions once in a while. However, if you constantly keep score on what people do or do not for you. For example, if a friend missed your birthday, anniversary or ditched your child's party, then the tendency is that you would the same also. This I'll-do-what-you-have-done-t me kind of attitude will eventually start make you a passive aggressive friend.

Another way of keeping score is asserting that you always have the worse or situation better. For instance, if a friend had a minor accident, a passive-aggressive friend would bring up a worse accident. If a colleague makes mention of a past recognition, a passive-aggressive friend would mention a better recognition.

The habit of keeping score will eventually weaken relationships. If you find yourself trying to recall what others have done to you in certain situations, then remind you that it is a clear example of a passive-aggressive behavior.

4. Have the tendency to give insincere compliment

When people are not happy about the pleasant things that happen to people around them but do not want to appear jealous or bitter about it, they would often give out insincere compliments. For example, if a female friend was proposed to, you may say, "I am happy for you," although deep down inside you actually feel bad her getting married before you do.

Another example is when you visit a friend's place, and instead of saying, " wow your place is small," you'd probably say, "it's cozy in here." These simple remarks, although common, are indicators of passive aggression. It would be better if you could take time before you utter your next words.

5. Have the tendency to put off tasks

Procrastination is one of the key indicators of passive aggression. This is considered one of most active forms and is often seen as mere laziness. Being unhappy with your current situation, whether personal or professional, may force you to deliberately delay projects, put off meetings, and care less about any activity within the day.

Procrastination can also manifest socially. Backing out last minute of events, not responding on time with invitations and constantly giving unnecessary excuses are all examples of how to one person can be passive aggressive even without meaning to do so. Examples of these excuses are not being able to read the e-mail, the invitation getting lost in the mail, your phone being lost or misplaced, etc.

If you catch yourself constantly making such excuses, it is about time to ponder on it and make certain changes. Then slowly make changes in your habit by promptly saying 'yes' or 'no' when invitation or event comes.

6. Trying to sabotage someone at work

Sabotaging is one of the extreme means of expressing passive aggression. This often happens at a workplace when someone tends to make decisions that could hurt another person professionally. For example, when an urgent memo had to disseminate, but you did not send it to a particular person, that is clearly a way of sabotaging him or her. When someone points this out, the common excuses of passive aggressive people are:" Oh I am sorry, I didn't know what happened?" "How did that happen?" and "I am sorry, I really had no idea."

Sabotaging can also happen at a personal level. For example, when you invite someone out for a drink when you know he is busy preparing for an exam or when you innocently give someone a packet of cigarette when he is actually trying to quit. Being instrumental to someone's downfall is a clear sign of having a passive aggressive behavior.

If you believe that you have the strong tendency to perform or display any of the aforementioned habits, it is highly recommended that you start reaching to people to validate and to better understand your habits. This will enable you to improve your level of sensitivity and to become more thoughtful and tactful with your words and actions.

Chapter 8: Modern Methods to Address Passive Aggression

Family and art can be instrumental in addressing problems linked with disorders such as Passive Aggression. It can be inferred that a huge number of people with behavioral disorders are still more comfortable dealing with their issues with the help of family members and things they are more passionate about.

Family Therapy

Family Therapy is a method that is usually considered when a certain malfunction exists within the family. The 'malfunctioning' aspect encompasses the general ability of a certain family to perform as a whole unit. It is now considered as one of the vital factors of any specific comprehensive method used to treat eating disorders such as Anorexia, Bulimia, Depression and Passive Aggression. There has been a series of recent researches that strengthen the effectiveness of this therapy in managing the said disorders. Family Therapy is also now becoming more and more popular as it can also applied in treating various medical and psychological disorders linked with sadness, anxiety, depression, guilt, jealousy, hatred and confusions.

Essential Components of this therapy include:

- Relationship Education
- Systems Theory
- Psych education
- Psychotherapy
- Attachment –focused therapy
- Reality Therapy
- Communications theory
- Media and communications theory

These diverse techniques are used to also help the patient endure a long counseling method, which may be necessary depending on the severity of his or her case.

Art Therapy

Art Therapy has also long been used in the aim to use creative art as a vehicle for cure and treatment. Media and the art are both used as communication channels for those dealing with psychological and psychiatric stress.

Art has been utilized to help individuals, particularly those dealing with shame and guilt brought about by eating disorders, to express their emotions and hidden concerns. The therapy is also known to be helpful in decreasing fear, anxiety, and stress. This therapy was first used in the middle of 20th century when Adrian Hill, an artist, learned about the therapeutic advantages of different art forms.

Art therapy also comes in various forms such as Painting, Drawing, Sculpting, Creating Mosaics, and Clay Making.

Essential Components of this therapy include:

- Road Drawing- an intervention that makes high use of metaphors to develop a tangible presentation of the patient's life;

- The Mandala Assessment Research Instrument (also referred to as Mari) – a technical procedure that involves the usage of different symbols, colors, legends, to make clear assessment of a patient's current and previous psychological condition;

- House-Tree-Person (also known as HTP)- an assessment instrument that is mainly used to evaluate a patient's personality via interpretation of different drawings

- The Diagnostic Drawing Series (more commonly known as DDS) – tool for clinical and diagnostic use.

Art Therapy should not also be confused with a regular art class. The therapy requires psychological guidance and interpretation from a team of expert. Each line, color, or figure are used to 'crack the code' on the specific problem pushing the patient to behave in an abnormal manner.

Cognitive Behavioral Therapy (CBT)

Function. CBT is a form of therapy that focuses on the interpretation of thinking patterns that may be distorted and irrational. Using psychodynamic procedures, symptoms can be easily dealt with. The main principle behind CBT is anchored in the idea that feelings and general thoughts are always linked with behavior. The main goal of CBT is wake the patient through the means of regaining control over the environment that will consequently ensure improvement of thinking patterns and behavior. CBT covers the understanding of overwhelming circumstances and breaking them down to allow management and reconnection. These facets include situations, emotions, actions, thoughts, and physical feelings.

Components of CBT

Stage #01: The Functional Analysis where the participant or patient is taught to identify his or her own problematic perceptions and beliefs

Stage#02: The Actual Behaviors Analysis is the phase where a new skill set is learned and practiced, and consequently applied to real-life situations

Stage# 03: The Behavior Change Stage is the finale where the patients are encouraged to take real measures in implementing their individual developmental transformation.

Different Types of CBT Therapy

Type #01: *Behavior Therapy* that focuses on the training an individual's reaction to stimuli; this also focuses on the treatment of any neurotic symptoms

Type #02: *Rational Emotive* that focuses on identifying and resolving behavioral disturbances

Type #03: *Cognitive Therapy* that aims to eradicate the negative patterns of thinking

Type #04: *Multimodal Therapy* that gives chief importance to interpersonal and sensation relationships

Maudsley Method Family Therapy

Function. Maudsley Method is an intensive outpatient treatment that allows people suffering from any eating disorder to be helped primarily by parents. The approach is specifically helpful for young sufferers of the Passive Aggression Disorder and was first formulated by a group of British specialists in Maudsley Hospital led by Dr. Christopher Dare. The treatment differs from other known approaches, as it also requires families to have a meal together under the supervision of a specialist or a psychiatrist. The meal shared as well as the interactions during the meal is recorded to further analyze the impact and the progress made by the sufferer. The reactions of the person who is passive aggressive is likewise recorded for further evaluation.

The Three Phases of the Maudsley Method

Phase #01: Establishment of thinking patterns. In this phase, the therapist aims to fully comprehend the various impacts of negative pattern of thinking, especially on the areas of cognitive, emotional, and physiological.

Phase #02: Regaining of Control. The phase aims to teach the patient to have healthier control over his responses and speaking habits.

Phase #03: Identity Re-establishment. This is the last phase of the treatment and is performed when the individual becomes mindful and healthy enough to recognize his own lapses. The management of the psychological impacts of the behavioral issue remains that primary focus of the stage. The patient will be strictly monitored until she or he is able to regain a healthier identity for him or herself.

Acceptance and Commitment Therapy (ACT)

Function.   One of the most recent therapies established is the Acceptance and Commitment Therapy, otherwise known as the ACT.   This therapy is associated with the idea of linking experiential avoidance to the psychological distress a person may experience. This therapy is somewhat the opposite of CBT as it focuses on the observation, recognition, and acceptance or private events.

ACT was first developed by a group of specialists namely Kelly Wilson, Kirk Strosahl, and Steven Hayes. The group aims to help people a psychological disorder such as those suffering from Passive Aggression, Depression, Anorexia, and Bulimia to attain better clarity and linkage to their personal values.

Five Phases of the Acceptance and Commitment Therapy (ACT)

Phase #01: Cognitive Defusing or the stage where strategies are discovered that would help lessen the tendency to put in place the negative images, thoughts, emotions

Phase #02: Acceptance or the stage where negative thoughts may be permitted without having to struggle with their presence

Phase #03: Contacting Realities or the stage where the patient develops mindfulness, sincerity, and openness to treatment

Phase #04: Self-observation or the stage where patient is taught how to retrieve an inspiring version of himself or herself

Phase #05: Values or the stage where one learns to accept the most significant facet of the individual's life

Phase #06: Commitment to act or the stage where goals to carry out actions to change and overcome the disorder are prioritized and reaffirmed.

Acceptance and Commitment Therapy is likewise carried out using three significant techniques namely Mindfulness therapy, Awareness-Management, and Cognitive Shifting Method.

Exposure and Response Prevention Therapy (ERP)

Exposure Response Prevention Therapy is among

techniques that aim to treat anxiety disorders that could lead to Passive Aggression. It may be seen as a radical approach as the person will be exposed to the object or circumstance that triggers his or her anxiety. The main goal of this technique is to desensitize the patient to his fears and stressors. The treatment usually lasts between 14 and 16 weeks, depending on the response of the patient.

The Different Types of ERP

Type #01: Gradual Exposure Therapy. Patients are gradually exposed to the stimuli during the sessions

Type #02: Prolonged Exposure Therapy. Patients are exposed much longer to see how much they can endure the stress and anxiety

Type#03: Exposure therapy Post Traumatic Stress Disorder (PTSD). This is specifically offered to patients who specifically want to heal from a certain event that may have triggered Post Traumatic Stress Disorder.

Type #04: Exposure Therapy Social Anxiety. This therapy aims to treat the patient's anxiety triggered by specific social events.

Chapter 9: Zapping the Habit of Procrastinating

Risking productivity and employment are just two of the direct impacts of procrastination. This is one of the most habits of someone inflicted with passive aggressive behavior. This is one habit that is likely experienced by people who are not so keen on following timetables, deadlines, and are a bit insensitive to the potential impacts of their habits. Again, procrastination is one of the most difficult habits to break.

So how do you combat procrastination? How do you refocus? What should you do understand the complications and consequences of procrastination? These questions can all be answered by first acknowledging that you do have the problem. Once you have done it then you can follow the following tips:

Efficient Ways to Getting Rid of Procrastination

- Start with a macro, work with the micro

This is how to set your goals. Start with what you would like to achieve for the whole week, and specify what you need to achieve for one whole day to achieve the bigger goal. Never rely on a big goal all the time as this would automatically crumble if you do not get to complete what you needed to finish in an hour or a day.

People who work from home have to learn the art of goal setting. Otherwise, with all the distractions that come with teleworking, none will be done at the end of the day. For example for writers, they can start with a 1000-word entry everyday and one chapter per week. Being very specific with your goal lets you understand the importance of small output and how they contribute to bigger results. By understanding the role of your output, you will be able to protect the result and avoid expressing any passive aggression to other people you work with.

- Make a schedule and with all your might, stick to it.

The absence of schedule is one of the reasons that

make procrastination possible. To avoid this, literally pen down your schedule and be very specific with the activities you are aiming to complete within the hour. If you find it a bit difficult to work for long periods, squeeze it a few minutes of break every two hours. Say a 15-minute break for every 2 hours of work. This will reduce the chances of your getting fed up with the work and ensures output. By understanding your schedule, you will be able to avoid sabotaging the timetable of others and learn to become more cooperative.

- Do not rely on the idea that you can always cram successfully

Learn how to pre-commit. It is always important to know what the potential consequences of cramming are. As a student, cramming would often work as it gives you the notion of not having any other way out. There are consequences, but not as serious as the repercussions of cramming at work as you are putting your general means of living at risk. There are now modern tools that let you stick to your goals and to follow your schedule.

- Get back to the old-fashioned way of writing down a 'to-do' list

Grab your pen and a sheet of paper and write down what you need to accomplish within the day. A passive-aggressive person would only pen this items down into their brain, but a productive person would instantly take the time to use write down the things they need to finish on a daily and weekly basis. Passive-aggressive people do not have this habit, which leads them to believe that they would always have the time to finish their tasks. Most of the time, they fail to do accomplish things or they had to sacrifice other tasks. This habit will not help you move up the ranks.

- Try to modify your work environment

See what is around you. If you habitually procrastinate then maybe there is something in your environment that makes you delay your work. For instance, does our workstation have so many accessories that remind you of your home. Is your neck or back pillow just too comfortable. Do you have a lot of photos of your kids that make you stop your work and head home instead? These are minor elements that could have a major impact on your productivity. Thus, these elements also fuel your passive aggression. Get rid of them and make your work space a true place for work.

- Deactivate Facebook and Twitter from your work computer

Yes, checking your browsing history can likewise help you eliminate the possibilities of putting off another task. You will most likely discover that you are spending way too much time on social media. Seek help from your IT team and request to have these sites blocked. Many may think that this is too drastic. However, dealing with passive aggression and procrastination likewise requires extreme approach to fully change these behaviors. If it is truly deemed necessary to take these actions, then by all means, say 'adieu' to your FB friends, Twitter followers, and other procrastination pit stops

- Surround yourself with very productive people

Choose your company and make sure that these people inspire you to become just as productive as they are. People generally influence other people. For you to stop being passive aggressive, do your best to only spend time with people full of optimism and action. Look around your office and determine those who tirelessly do their job without having to complain or put off even the simplest task. Be inspired by people who constantly receive credits for a job well done. A good company helps modify our behavior.

- Get other people in the loop

To be able to fully understand how you behave, try to find a couple of people whom you can discuss your goals with. These people may help you avoid procrastinating by reminding you of your goals. Some people find it useful to print out their goals and post them in places where they would surely these reminders. Seeing these reminders also help you visualize a happy and successful future.

- Talk to someone

Reach to another person if you find yourself being too lax with your task. If you catch yourself being too comfortable with delays, then it is time to start talking about it to someone. Finding the right person may be a challenge, too. You may opt to talk to someone who had successfully completed the same task as yours. Another option is to also discuss your problem with someone who can bluntly remind you of your problems and delays.

- Just pull your weight- No but's and no excuses

The best way to fix this odd habit of procrastinating is to start moving. Start with your task and convince yourself to continue working. No matter how dragging it could get, let your body move and accomplish tasks little by little.

By the time you see your work progress, you may feel more motivated in the end.

Now, you know these simple steps on how put an end to your procrastinating habits; you may amplify the steps and get yourself an extra boost from apps and technology. Read on to learn how technology can help you resolve this problem.

Chapter 10: Productivity Apps and Boosters for the Passive-Aggressive

Passive Aggression gets in the way of productivity, and that is not healthy if it happens for a long period of time. Getting your way out of the procrastination spell needs a great deal of courage, motivation, and help. The more help you can get, the easier you can rebound from the curse of laziness and being demotivated.

How you ever caught yourself Tweeting incessantly during work hours? Have you caught yourself lurking on the Web and constantly checking what your FB friends have been up to lately? Well, it's time to change NOW before it is too late. See how technology can help you polish your behavior and get rid of the roughness of passive aggression in your everyday life.

Apps that Can Help Boost Your Productivity and Stop the Curse of Procrastination

Strict Workflow

This is a Google Chrome extension that lets you work for 25 minutes straight and gives you a 5-minute break. This is similar to the promodoro technique. The purpose is to allow you work without distraction and help you cultivate a habit that will guarantee output. The extension also automatically blocks sites such as Facebook, Twitter and YouTube. The timer can be easily activated by a single click on a button.

Productivity Owl

This tool is tantamount to having a personal and digital watcher that forces you to get back to your work. The tool follows your browsing habits and automatically closes the pages that may sidetrack you from work. It is also capable of blocking sites and resetting a timer. It follows the work schedule you input at the beginning. If you closely follow your schedule, you will eventually earn the 'respect' of the owl. This can only be used with Google Chrome.

Meet Carrot

Although the name sounds sweet and healthy, this app is actually 'sadistic' capable of calling the user mean names just to make him work and move. The app makes blunt remarks to ensure that you would do your task. It will track all your accomplishments and make nasty remarks if it in any case you fail to complete what you had to finish. It's 'sister' app called Carrot Fit does the same for people who fail to meet their weight loss goals.

Freedom

This app can be downloaded by Mac and Window. What it basically does is sets you free from any potential distractions from the web. For example, you will not be able to access the Internet for a good 45-minutes. You may also read just the timer, even up to 8 hours. The challenge is that you will not be able to make any adjustment at anytime. You will have to finish your task first. The app comes with a free trial. However, if you find it efficient, you will need to pay a minimal fee of $10 to download the premium version. This is not much for the amount of productivity you will gain.

Leechblock

For users of Mozilla Firefox, Leechblock can be your ultimate tool. As the other productivity tool, this app lets you work non-stop without getting sidetracked by websites such as Facebook, Twitter, and YouTube. The site lets you focus on your work between 9am up to 5pm. It also comes with a random code that will allow you to reset the schedule at any time you wish.

Stopdistractions

This is the ultimate anti-Facebook or anti-YouTube tool that passive aggressive people can use, particularly those use Windows PC. It automatically limits you access to certain sites. You may continue to use the Internet, however, for very important research. You can set your own work schedule, too.

Meettimer

This site does not really block sites that may be of distraction to you. Instead, it closely monitors your browsing habits and records how much time you spend on one specific site. It then prepares statistics that will help you understand your behavior online, which covers your surfing habits, time spent on a site interns of percentage, and the top sites you visit in one day. By doing so, you will be able to gather sufficient information that will help you modify your habits.

Instant Boss

This is the app for those people who have a much stronger willpower to follow a strict schedule. For example, for people who are able to function in a work-simulated schedule, the plugin Instant Boss can be particularly helpful. Once installed, you will receive constant pop ups when you can take a break and resume working. You will also receive notifications that will ask you to work overtime. Note that this application is specifically for Windows users.

Checklist Tools such as iOS Reminders, Evernote, Google Keep, and Workflowy

These tools remind of you of your objectives and expected output within a specific period. You can constantly check your to-do list as well as other tasks you need to be reminded of. To make it even more motivating, you may include in your to-do list the benefit of finishing such task.

Important Reminder about Using Productivity Tools

Apps and any Web tools cannot and will not do the work for you. They can help you become more strategic and polish you work behavior. More importantly, you cannot label any of these tools as ineffective or inefficient. It is always up to you and your eagerness to produce something that would really bring forward results and changes.

It is also advised that you only use these tools within a specific period of time. Hopefully, after a month or two, you will be able to embody the mindset of a highly productive person and a non-passive aggressive colleague. It is likewise expected that by using these tools, you will be able to enjoy a more dependable self.

Chapter 11: Confronting the Passive-Aggressive the Healthy Way

Passive Aggression exists in almost all kinds of relationship – personal, marriage, familial, work, social, even political. While it is often perceived as a strategy to avoid confrontations, the most radical yet effective manner of addressing the problem is by confronting the situation and the person. This is to avoid the occurrence of long-term issues. Therefore, some experts would likewise recommend people to become a bit more aggressive actively to put an end of the repercussions of such behavioral matter. Knowing how they shown such passive aggression can also help you spot the issue more easily.

In order to sustain a much healthier relationships at work and at home and to ensure assertive communications, experts recommend the following healthy strategies in confronting such behavior.

1. **Become more sensitive to the warning signs of passive aggression**

Passive aggression may seem subtle for some. However, it is important to keep in mind that such behavior is actually deliberately executed by people who find comfort in masking their own feelings. This is also described as a manner of expressing feelings of anger. The hostility, stubbornness, and even abrupt laziness that come with it are all used to hide the true feeling of anger.

People who are quickly able to discern real hostility from merely sugarcoated anger; they tend to have the opportunity to disengage as quickly as possible. This is the first critical step that will save both the giver and the receiver of the behavior from a bleaker relationship. To understand the common signs of passive aggression, go back and review what you have learned from Chapter 7.

2. **Never let passive aggression get to you**

Passive-aggressive people will do their best to get to your nerves without being too obvious about it.

The lack of engagement will enable you to protect yourself from the destructive behavior of a passive-aggressive. Moro ever, you will also be able to help the other person by making him realize that such behavior will not give him the satisfaction he wants. To help you fight back the unnecessary confrontation, you may literally speak to yourself say, " Ok, he is just being passive-aggressive. This is not about me and I will not let him make me part of his problem."

3. **Be direct so passive aggression will not escalate whatever conflict there is**

One characteristic of passive-aggressive people is their inability to be direct. They are also unable to acknowledge anger. If you feel that you have constantly been a victim of endless display of passive-aggression, you can use this weakness to your advantage. The next time, the passive-aggressive gets to you, you can directly say, "I am sorry you feel that way and it seems that you are angry at me because... ". Hearing these words will essentially help them reaffirm their feelings and eventually address their anger correctly.

However, you may also expect that the person would deny it at first. If this is the case, then you can be more specific as to why you feel he or she is being passive-aggressive. He will eventually run out of excuses and will slowly open up and become more honestly with his feelings. You will be able to teach him a thing or two by being the overly honest one.

4. **Trust your instincts**

Recognizing the behavioral pattern of a passive-aggressive person is easier than most people think. The messages they send through their words and reactions will automatically help you distinguish the problematic areas. At some point, you will need to react. There is standard or straightforward approach when dealing with a passive-aggressive person. Most of the time, you need to trust what your gut tells you. Whatever reaction you may have, this will bring out a realization on their end that can be instrumental for them to becoming more open and honest about their feelings.

5. **Remembering you do not deserve such treatment**

You are human and you just happened to be surrounded by other humans of different personalities. The different characteristics are expected. However, being treated differently by the passive-aggressive people is not healthy and never OK. If another person constantly shows hostility and stubbornness, it is important to let yourself know that such treatment should never be tolerated. Muster up the courage and ask, " I hope we can talk about what your problem really is, so we can avoid conflicts as I do not want one." Being able to use such words will help the other person understand that you are not taking the backseat with his behavior.

To confront the passive-aggressive is never easy, but can be done. The moment you let the other person know that you KNOW about her characteristics can be a good way to cut yourself lose from the bullying, hostility and aggression. If you constantly encounter this at the workplace, read the next chapter to see how you can cope.

Chapter 12: Defusing Passive Aggression in the Workplace

We all have that list of people we just really love to hate at work. Let's be brutally honest about it – some colleagues are just way too annoying to work with. Although it is not really encourages to hate someone we spend 8-10 hours a day with, no one can, Although it working with unpleasant people – those who give us the cold stare at the lift or the hallway, the master procrastinator, the people who do not pull their weight for some reason, the stubborn, and the overly negative one. In short, the passive-aggressive colleague who we will never get used to working with.

If you happen to work with a person that displays any of the aforementioned behavior 'naturally', then it is safe to say that you have to deal with an angry person on a daily basis. For managers, this becomes a more difficult and sensitive situation. They cannot react, particularly if they are keen on following a compassionate style of management. Being mindful of their action is also one of the challenges. But overall, this has to change. So how do you manage a team when one member tends to be ticking emotional bomb waiting to explode? How do you control potential damage? How do you address a passive-aggressive person without being one?

Whilst we may have all experience passive-aggression from a loved one, relative, or a friend, having to deal with it in a workplace creates a whole new scenario. After all, business is at stake. Your profession is at stake, too. Here are some steps on how you can defuse a ticking passive-aggression bomb at work:

1. Never take the bait. The passive aggressive person would want to see you explode at some point. They assume that you will eventually reach the boiling point and will make you appear the real bad person in the scenario. Remember this and keep yourself from being the victim. Do not take their actions as a personal level. It's work related so you should not thinking about such behavior at home. Never let aggression take over your peace of mind.'

2. Make sure that you always keep a safe distance. If it is not necessary, just try to keep yourself away from the view of a passive-aggressive person. Never attempt to please them, as you will not be able to do so. The passive-aggressive is an angry person and it is not easy to pacify an angry person who is in denial about. Unless it is urgent or work-related, then do not bother entering his personal space.

3. Avoid passing the ball to the other person. As much as you can, try not to delegate important work to this person. At least, when you know he is still unable to cast his anger aside. This will just put your work at risk. If he thinks he is not being considered well enough at work, then let him approach you instead.

4. Keep calm and stay collected. 'Wear' this slogan at all times. You will not be able to resolve anything if you play fire against fire. Put yourself in a strong position by not uttering any unnecessary words. Make silence your powerful weapon and try to use to motivate your team further.

5. When addressing a problem with a specific person, get 'involved' in the problem. This will eliminate the feeling of being the victim. For instance, instead of saying, " You have done this," you may want to rephrase it with, " We reached this point." This will eventually pacify their anger and make them feel more at ease little by little.

6. Ponder on their behavior. Remember the rule of action and reaction? Maybe you can check on that, too. Reflect on their behavior by asking yourself, " Have I turned you into..?" " Do I do the same thing?" "What have I done this past month" "What have I positively contributed to his work?" These questions will help you see areas that were maybe difficult for you to see when at work.

7. Talk to others. Know how they feel about working together. Understand the usual causes of conflict on your team. Are they having the same problem? Have you been fair to everyone? Ask your subordinates three things that they like about their job and three other thinks that they do not. You may connect certain ideas here and find out the root cause of the passive aggression.

8. Use humor whenever possible. By showing that you are one positive person can help you discover the positive site of your colleagues, too. This is helpful when understanding the behavior of someone with passive aggression. Does he react well to compliments? Does he laugh at your jokes? Does he try to be alone all the time? Know the answer to these questions and find out about the habits and behavior of the person.

9. Cordon the passive- aggressive person from others. If possible, try to make this person on a solo project. This will avoid him from having any more victims with this behavior and therefore resolve the toxic behavior at work. It is important

not to let other people get exposed with the behavior, too.

10. Ask for solutions, too. Passive-aggressive people always point out what is wrong. Instead of focusing on the problem, let them know that you are interested on their output, too. Ask for suggestions and keep their ideas.

You cannot always resolve a conflict easily, but you must always give them a try. It is essential to also add a dash of patience when working with these people.

Chapter 13: A Self Check on the Many Faces of Passive Aggression

Passive aggression can turn be a tough call for all – to both the aggressor and the victim. Among friends, it can be a reason for conflict. Within a family, it can be enough to tear siblings apart. At work, it can be the reason for failure. In short, passive aggression is never easy to deal with. If you were ever called passive-aggressive, it is appropriate for you to do some thinking and reevaluate yourself and your behavior. This is vital so you can make the necessary changes that will save your relationships with other people. So what kind of passive-aggressive are you? Read on and find out.

Are you the BULLY?

Bullying is always about being overly aggressive over someone. The worst kinds of bullies are those who can intimidate passively. They can demean others by using words that may intimidate others. They can harass others without looking mean. In short, these are the passive-aggressive that find joy in making feel inferior.

How to deal with the BULLY: Never show fear when they are present. These people can smell 'fear' and let them know that you can stand up for yourself, too.

Are you the MASTER PROCRASTINATOR?

You may also be called master slacker. If you only pull your weight when it benefits you or when you try to intentionally slow down the workflow that could impact the performance of the whole team, then it is safe to conclude that you are, indeed, a passive-aggressive kind of colleague. The worst kinds of procrastinator are those who can subtly influence others to behave the same way. These people are usually those who are burnt out or who already feel left out in the career cycle. People who are unfairly treated at work may lead to becoming a master slacker themselves.

How to deal with the MASTER PROCRASTINATOR: Show them the consequences of not completing the task. It is also important to also make them see the long-term results of their behavior. Most procrastinators do not feel threatened about their work and so confidently slack off at work.

Are you the IDEA BUSTER?

Do you like answering with a bit of sarcasm? Do you constantly see the negative outcome before the positive? Do you hate hearing other people's ideas? Do you run out of ideas to share? If you answer YES to all these questions, then yes, you are the idea busting kind of passive aggressive.

How to deal with the IDEA BUSTER: If such behavior escalate, then instead of brainstorming, you may want to seek for people's ideas through writing and let them react non-verbally, too. By limiting the meetings temporarily, the idea busters will not have the opportunity to send out negativity towards other people.

Are you the TATTLETALE?

Do you like reporting to the bosses about the simplest things? This is one of ways the passive-aggressive people ruins the atmosphere at work. The idea of being the reporter at work gets in the way of healthy relationships. The tattletale also has the tendencies to letting the people in top management about the mishaps of his team or the mistakes made by direct managers. These people are usually jealous of other people's accomplishment and so they find ways to tarnish their good records.

How to deal with the TATTELETALE: These people usually get the hint upon receiving a kind of silent treatment from colleagues. Deliberately excluding them on some occasions will make them realize that they behavior is certainly frowned upon by colleagues.

Are you the GOSSIP?

Everyone hates this behavior, but sadly most people enjoying being one. The gossipers just like to talk about everything unnecessary and negative about some people. They create factions easily and are a champion in ruining relationships. They hate being the subject, but love being the storyteller. These are also among the top-notch passive-aggressive people who are unable to release their frustration openly.

How to deal with the GOSSIP: Never engage. A person who likes to listen to a gossip has generally a weak personality. Stand up and be blunt about not being able to stomach to talk about other people's lives. They need to be rejected to stop the behavior.

Are you the HARASSER?

These are people who use gestures that generally result in fear, intimidation, and humiliation. People of higher ranks or seniors in a company have the tendency to become one once they see someone with full potential in the workplace. They usually like mixture of races in a workplace, working with entry-level employees, teaming up with the opposite sex or people from a different department.

How to deal with the HARASSER: Being a victim of harasser gives you every right to discuss the matter with your HR manager. There is never a reason to be harassed in any way – verbally, non-verbally, and sexually. The passive-aggressive people will always look at this as a way to get ahead of the pack. Never let this happen and be vocal about the harassment you experience at work.

Are you the ULTIMATE PERFECTIONIST?

Everybody wants to produce accurate output. However, some passive-aggressive people tend to put perfectionism to a higher level. These are the people who always have something to say even when things work very well. They like to point out even the smallest, most negligible imperfection of the work. They find joy in creating conflicts at work. Most of the time, they like to speak about how they would approach a project if they had to work on it alone.

How to deal with the ULTIMATE PERFECTIONIST: Take note of the real output and not the accomplishments they imagine they would have. Make them understand that goals and results are the two primary parameters of a successful project. Remind them that then imperfections will also be addressed during the evaluation and quality inspection. Lastly, remind of their specific role in a project.

Are you the NARCISSIST?

The narcissist hate to be left out and they use sarcasm and silence to protest. They tend to be extremely sensitive when their ideas get rejected or when not recognized. These are the typical behavior of egocentric and narcissistic type of passive-aggressive.

How to deal with the NARCISSISTIC: Be generous with praises ONLY when they deserve it. Make their efforts known and thank them for their hard work. Moreover, make sure that you give them sufficient workload so they could focus more on the work and not just on the output. Engaging them to group activities would also help them realize the importance of the working collaboratively and also to make them see the importance of working with others.

These all represent the FACES of people who are passive-aggressive. They are generally unable to express their anger and resentment. Therefore, they have the tendencies to conceal their behaviors and show the following faces instead. If you find yourself behaving in any way discussed above, then it is best to start seeking ways to free yourself from this kind of aggression. The rest of the book will help your break away from the chains of passive aggression.

Chapter 14: Eradicating Passive Aggression through Refocusing

Passive Aggression can break relationships. Moreover, they can hinder you from achieving your personal goals. The behavior tends to distract you from your real goals. Your anger can sidetrack you from taking the right path to success. How do you change your fate?

Though it sounds rather simple, the best way for you to achieve your dreams is to get rid of passive aggression and learn to refocus. By refocusing, you will be able to see the things that are more important and worthy of your time. By learning how to focus again, you will not only get rid of passive aggression, but you will also be able to learn how to identify the other roadblocks to your success. The question now is --- how do we start?

Refocusing begins with re-evaluation of your goals

Due to passive aggression, people tend to forget about these goals and get driven by their anger instead. When this happens, the expression of angers becomes more important that the result of hard work and effort. This is why passive aggression is considered a powerful way to fail. It blinds people from their real targets and reestablishes a different set of goals that are not helpful for them in any way.

Here are some of the tips on how you can reevaluate your goals:

- Write your goals again. You may have already done this at the beginning; you need to start from scratch in order for you to make all the necessary changes. By rewriting your goals, you will be able to understand your priorities again.

- Come up with a new timeline. Do not waste your emery grieving over the wasted time. You do not have the time for this now. Establish a timetable and write down your expected output. Make sure that you do not omit any step.

- Understand where your 'breaking point' was. Passive aggression results from anger that stemmed from a failure. Find out what triggered your breaking point and what caused you to behave differently. Was a failed project? Were you pushed by a mean comment? Did your efforts go to waste? These can contribute to your change of behavior.

- Speak with a colleague and honestly ask him about your change in behavior. Be ready to hear the meanest comments, but remind yourself the purpose of this process. Use these comments to track the triggering factors of your passive aggression.

Restart by taking baby steps again. Do not force yourself to change all at once. It will never happen and it will just put all your efforts in vain. Start from step one and take note of your achievements. Try to minimize interactions with others if it will not help you achieve your goals.

Take some breathers. Refocusing can be done if your mind and body are at one. This means that a tired body or a tired mind can instantly distract you. If you are tired, you may want to take a 5-minute break. Otherwise, you may just find yourself staring into space the rest of the day.

Do a daily check of your achievement. Whether it is just a small achievement or a major accomplishment, write them down and commend yourself for such achievement. See this pattern grow until it becomes a habit of yours.

Show expression of gratitude. Thanking others and showing gratitude to people who have helped you in completing a task can strengthen your refocusing habits. This will help you also reestablish your relationships with others, which would be helpful in the long-term.

Changing is never easy. Modifying your habits and trying to mend broken relationships are sometimes impossible. However, making extra efforts to somehow improve yourself is always appreciated by others. This can also help you achieve the success you deserve.

Chapter 15: Eradicating Passive Aggression Through Meditation

Truth be told – passive aggression is not easy to deal with. But another truth be told – it can be fixed using natural methods such as meditation. For many people, resorting to passive aggression tends to be a more comfortable way to express anger. Why not? You can be angry without looking and sounding like one. You can express your feeling without having to be overly open about it. Sounds convenient, right? WRONG!

Using passive aggression to express anger, dislike, disappointment, etc. is a form of weakness. The kind of weakness that can easily drag you down. The kind of weakness that zaps productivity and puts your employment in danger. Worst, it is the kind of weakness that can easily repel people around you. You do not want to end up alone, unhappy, and angry, do you? Put a full stop on your passive aggression. Put a stop NOW.

Your behavior and your thoughts are just two of the facets of life that you can take full control of, only if you truly desire it. Meditation is also one of the most important teachings in Buddhism, which lets people deal with their emotions and sorrow by a method called meditation.

When you look at the big picture, fixing a habit or behavior may sound like a long shot. Well, it is — if you do not put your heart and soul to it. However, if you want to see yourself as new person, you will be open to options to do it. Get yourself ready and prepare your mind for a completely different way of eradicating passive aggression. Be open and ready to MEDITATE.

What is meditation?

Buddhists consider meditation as the way we restore human condition that is inflicted with hatreds, anger, fears, sorrows, confusions and anxieties. It is achieved by a complete transformation of the mind. Meditation requires techniques that generally require concentration leading to emotional positivity, clarity, and tranquility.

The practice of meditation lets you understand

the habits and patterns if your mind which will ultimately help you cultivate new thoughts, thinking pattern, and develop a more positive way if life. This can particularly helpful for those who are having difficulties changing their way of life such as people who tend to live with passive aggression. The transformation effect of meditation can help people deal with anger effectively.

Apart from the emotional healing it gives, meditation also lets you experience the following:

- manage and relieve stress effectively and safely
- improved focus, memory, happiness, performance, and self-control
- better heart rate, healthy respiration, normal blood pressure etc.
- a developed self-awareness
- a better expression of emotions

The next question is – how do we meditate? What are the techniques and how are they executed? A simplified method of meditation is now possible to help the beginners on their quest for a better version of themselves. If you are ready to embrace a better version of yourself through meditation, you can follow the following steps:

Step #01: Find the right spot. Make sure it is quiet, clean, and free from clutters. It is recommended that you start meditating early in the morning while everyone else is at sleep. A soothing corner in your home, part of the garden, or somewhere close to the beach is recommended. Your chosen spot should keep you away from people even just for a few minutes.

Step #02: Sit in a comfortable position. What you wear and what you sit on are not important. How comfortable you are in your position is what matters most. Lean against the wall or sit on a comfortable pillow. Some people find it best to sit in a cross-legged position while others tend to do the 'Indian' sitting position. Experienced mediators have also learned the art of sitting on a bare floor.

Step #03: Start with a few minutes of meditation. It is not mandatory to meditate for a long period of time. Start with just a few minutes. Sometimes practicing meditation for merely 5 minutes can produce the best results. This can be a good start. You can prolong the meditation period once you have started to develop the habit. The important thing with meditation is keeping the habit. The consistency will help you build a conscious mind and habits that are much easier to follow. For your second week of meditation, you can add 2-3 minutes, until you reach a point when meditating for 15-30 minutes becomes very easy.

Step #4: Focus on your breathing.

Imagine the oxygen getting through your system. Breathe in and feel the air coming to your lungs. Feel the movement of your stomachs. Sit straight and keep a post posture. You may opt to close your eyes, but keeping them open will open just fine. Once you breathe out, imagine the air going out of your system, too. Count as you let the air out. Count slowly. You may find yourself wandering at some point, and that is expected from beginners. Just try to get back to the breathing practice and you will be just fine.

You may expect some difficulties at the beginning, especially when you are the kind that is easily distracted. It is also not recommended to use music at the beginning. The primary purpose is to learn how to focus on breathing and not try to be clouded by anything. Once you learn to concentrate and stay still calmly, then you can start incorporating such as music to your routine. Perfecting the meditation techniques would help the passive-aggressive cultivate better behavior. They would be able to see more naturally the proper way to interact with others and to live without any sense of aggression.

Chapter 16: Eradicating Passive Aggression Through Elimination of Negative Thinking

Mind Power can be particularly powerful especially when trying to pacify passive aggression. This is also the ultimate tool in achieving any goals that are essential to your existence at home, at work, and in the general society. In a simplified definition, mind power generally means focusing on something you want which you will eventually attract. This also means that you are capable of training your mind to only focus on the things the matter to you the most. For example, if you want to eliminate fear, anger, and negative thinking, you can by using your mind power.

People inflicted with passive-aggression generally live with anger that they are not able to express. By eliminating the thought, you can help yourself regain control of yourself and deliberately avoid making conflicts at home and at home by being aggressive passively.

So how can you exactly eliminate these negative thoughts? How do you begin reliving a better, conflict-free life? How can you finally say 'adieu' to passive-aggression?

To successfully eliminate negative thoughts such as anger, you will first have to know and acknowledge the importance of getting of them. Secondly, you will have to learn how to recognize when anger starts to happen to you.

It is important to also emphasize that this is not a very easy exercise, but it is worth all the effort you put to it. While it is true that negative thought can just simply cross our mind, you still have the power to alter it by recognize how 'bad' the though it. Once you have become better at recognizing the negative thoughts that position your mind, you can then apply the following techniques:

1. Replace the negative idea with a positive thought. Let's say you remember getting reprimanded by your boss, immediately think of what you can do to make things right instant. You will feel a sudden jolt of joy once you are able to replace the old thought. Remember that as humans, we can only entertain one thought at a time. So if you are

able to refocus on a more positive idea, you are already able to get rid of the negative thought.

2. Hold on to the positive thought by using a strong affirmation. Constantly remind yourself of this positive thought. Strengthen the presence of this positive by thinking of it repeatedly. Thinking out loud would also help.

3. When the negative thought tries to pin you down, divert your attention to something fun or humorous. For instance, if you are passive-aggressive and you feel like to being sarcastic to someone, simply go back to your computer and read a funny story. This will help you change your thought until you feel better again.

4. Constantly remind yourself that 'a thought is just a thought', nothing more. Become more proactive in belittling the power of negative thought over you. You are still the master of your mind and you can alter it any time you wish. Take appropriate measures when your surrounding reminds of anything negative. Go to other places. See other people. Do not hesitate to explore options when trying to overpower your negative thoughts.

Negative thoughts such as those filled with anger lead to a very toxic mind. Trying to live day-by-day with a negative thought can automatically turn you to a negative person. Positive thoughts breed positive people. Negative thoughts aggravate passive aggression.   Use your mind power to shield yourself from adverse effects of passive aggression.

Chapter 17: Eradicating Passive Aggression Through Breathing Exercises

It is never easy to deal with passive aggression – the stress it brings, the negativity it causes, and the extra effort it requires to approach a person inflicted with it, can all take a toll on you. The demands of your work and of your daily life add to the things you need to deal with on a daily basis. Sometimes, it feels that everything is too much to handle. Sometimes, it is.

The emotional and psychological exhaustion brought about by passive aggression becomes unbearable overtime. So how do you detoxify your mind and spirit? How do you start a day of trials and challengers? How do you keep yourself calm? These are the questions that inundate a person with passive-aggressive personality disorder as well as the people that surround him.

To free yourself from the hardships of passive aggression, all you need is to allow 10-15 minutes of your time performing meditation. Through this platform, you will be able to transform your mind and experience calmness, tranquility, and happiness from within. Overcoming the negative thinking pattern you have been accustomed to is also one of the end results of a good meditation.

The basic purpose of a brief meditation is to free the mind from the mental toxins that generate anger, worries, discomfort, and sadness. With an angry mind, it is surely difficult to be happy. When you live with anger, you are unable to connect to people and create healthy relationships.

The mind of a passive-aggressive person is comparable to a balloon that is easily filled by negativity. Once full, it flies away making it difficult to contain or hold again. Through meditation, the person will be able to learn how to pop the balloon immediately before the wind controls it. Clearing what is inside of it is the only way to remove the aggression. Through meditation, he will be able to see things different and more positively.

While you may say that 'it is so much easier said

than done', meditation is highly achievable. This is also one of the most important teachings of the Buddhists. The process of meditation is process by which we learn how to free ourselves from the delusions that trigger anger, suffering, and hardships. Being able to practice it regularly will help us achieve permanent happiness that will be shared by people around you.

Beginners may find it a little difficult to perform breathing exercises the first time. However, it takes practice and training to be able to meditate deeply. One of the simplest and most recommended forms of meditation is the one that involves breathing exercise. Here are the following steps:

1. Find a quite place where you can regularly meditate. The spot should be free from distraction for a good 20 minutes every day. It can be in one corner of your room, in your terrace, your favorite spot in the garden, or anywhere close to a fountain or beach. The sound of water can be particularly therapeutic. Check the area and see how far it is from the next area frequented by people. Look around the area and be connected with the surrounding. Do this before the first day of your meditation. Understand where sounds and the win come from. Feel the area by touching the floor, the sitting area, and the elements around. Be one with the spot.

2. Wake up extra early for your first meditation. It is recommended that you do the meditation before everyone else in your home wake up. Sit comfortably for a few minutes. You may sit on a chair or a cushion on the floor. Some people also prefer to sit directly onto the bare floor. Others cross their legs while others like to have them stretched. Keep your posture straight, but feel comfortable throughout. You may keep your eyes open or closed. Do not get distracted by your surroundings. Bear in mind that there is only you in that moment. Do not be overly comfortable, as you may feel sluggish or sleepy afterwards. Note that with meditation, your mind should stay awake but focused.

3. Take a deep breath and breathe out slowly. Count one to ten as you breathe in and breathe out. Feel the air entering your system and feel your gut move as you take in air and expel it out. Follow the movement of the air. Do not rush it. Count slowly and stay focused on your routine. If you somehow get distracted and lost count, try to pull yourself in again and restart counting. First-timers may find this part difficult but it will become easier and easier eventually.

4. Do the breathing meditation for 5 minutes for your first week. Prolong the routine as you go further. A good 20-minutes should be enough when you have already built the routine. While

some find it useful to listen to meditation music, it is advised that beginners should only listen to their counting and the sound of their breath.

5. Make it a habit to meditate at the start of the day and before you sleep at night. This will help you get rid of the worries you have during the day. This will empty your mind and ready it for another day. Take note of your progress and be kind enough to share the positive effects of meditation in your life. Create a circle of positive people.

For people with personality disorder such as passive aggression, a few minutes a day is all it takes to change the way of their thinking. If seeing a shrink becomes a challenge more than a cure, then the other efficient way to use the mental power you have to change the way you think, feel and behave towards other people.

The passive people will also be able to benefit from meditation in several ways. One is that meditation can strengthen their self-control. This is particularly helpful in managing aggressive behavior. Another benefit is that it lets people to have an overall better health that includes healthier heart rate, more stable blood pressure, and fewer headaches.

Chapter 18: Eradicating Passive Aggression Through Visualization Techniques

Apart from eliminating negative thinking pattern and practicing meditation, another way to resolve passive aggressive personality disorder is through the application of visualization techniques.

Though it sounds technical, this approach is no longer new to many people. In fact, a lot of people use the process of visualizing gaining advantage in a particular situation. For example, for someone who is about to do the presentation of his lifetime may use visualization to gain confidence and to anticipate the questions. Athletes do the same to motivate themselves and keep them in the zone of the game. Basically, visualization lets people experience the situation they fear, expect, excited about, in order to know how they can behave when that situation comes.

For people living with passive aggression, being around other people offers them the opportunity to show the subtle aggression. If you believe that you are becoming this kind of person, then you can do something to change your behavior though the technique. For example, you may visualize having a wonderful lunch with colleagues or being able to discuss with someone openly. Another situation that a person working with passive aggressive colleagues can practice on is the ability to ask directly about a particular problem. One can also visualize the kind of output he wants to attain.

There are different visualization techniques that people with behavioral problems can use to simplify and improve their lives. They may choose any of the following techniques:

Receptive Type of Visualization – This is the kind of visualization technique that is easiest to perform. This is comparable to creating a scene as though directing a movie. The person visualizing has full control of the scenes, the dialogues, as well as the outcome in the end. Whether you are the person dealing with passive aggressive behavior or the person inflicted with it, you can apply the scenarios you are most afraid of, and then visualize a positive result. You can slowly add one image at a time until you complete the story you wish to experience. This will help you gain the confidence to face the same situation in the future.

Treasure Map Type of Visualization – This technique involves physical and mental components to set up the scenarios you wish to have. This requires an extra effort by drawing the result you wish to achieve. For instance, if working with passive aggressive people becomes a hurdle at work, you can draw your group holding hands. You may also want to produce a graphic presentation of the results you wish to have at the end of the year. Make the drawings as detailed as possible. As you add each line, curve, letters, you can start mentally visualizing the positive side of the scenario. This technique requires a great deal of patience, as it will take time before the person can fully submerge in the idea. Looking at the photo will help them physically see the areas they want to dominate and change. It is advised that this technique be performed in the quietest area within the room.

Altered Memory Technique of Visualization- This technique helps people come to terms with regrets or with events they can never change in real life. However, with visualization, they will be able to understand a past experience better. By recreating it, the anger or regrets will eventually. Once you recreate the scenario, you may alter the angry responses you gave with something calmer and more controlled. This will prompt you to become more controlled in the future. Thus, passive aggression can be managed well.

Meditation. This generally lets you reach a calm and peaceful place where you can displace all the anger and anxieties you have been dealing with. Through meditation, you will be able to start a new day with clear mind and more controlled emotions. This process will also let you heal all the emotional wounds you have been living with. It's a self-healing process that even people with passive aggressive behavior can utilize.

Chapter 19: Managing Passive-Aggressive Kids

Passive Aggression is not only a mechanism demonstrated by adults. Kids-- even those as young as 5 years old can already be inflicted by such behavior disorder. The first few signs of passive aggression in kids include the difficulty to call at the dining room, the resistance they show when you ask them to do simple things, the lack of interest when you try to tell them off, or when they refuse to pick up their toys after playing.

Some parents may argue that these are just common behavior of kids. However, experts warn parents that these behaviors can already help the kids build the power to resist the parents. Although they do not talk back, yell back, or respond verbally, there is already an existing aggression building up in their system.

The Development of Passive Aggression in Kids

Sadly, many parents tend to blame themselves when their children turn out to be the opposite of what they expect. It is important to know that children grow differently, absorb learning in different ways, and get to be influenced in a number of ways. Passive aggression is one of the most challenging aspects that parents find difficult to deal with. Children who are becoming passive aggressive are already discovering ways to avoid expression of feelings or confrontation of anger. For instance, when a kid goes up in his room without even saying Hi to the parents is already a clear sign of concealment of feeling.

Common response you may get from kids suffering from passive aggressive behavior are: " Leave me alone, " "Stop saying that," " You do not need to that," and "Stop telling me what to do." When children are starting to ask for their space, it is usually passive aggression that prompts them to do so.

As they are kids and generally inexperienced, they find it difficult to discuss about their conflicts which lead them to becoming frustrated, hostile, and sometimes- extremely melancholic. If this pattern continues, the passive aggression is the behavior aggravated and is carried on throughout adulthood. Once this happens, a more serious set of conflicts awaits them at work and even in their personal relationships. When these adults become more resistant to people, they will eventually turn out to be the 'bad apples' in the bunch. In the end, even the most important relationships such as marriage and families, may start to crumble down. This is exactly why passive aggression should be immediately addressed in the childhood. Fixing it the soonest possible time will save your children from experiencing the worst kind of treatment when they grow older.

Knowing how to respond correctly to the children is absolute imperative to keep the passive aggression from developing and being applied even in the adulthood years. Experts also suggest that parents become utterly sensitive to the words of their children and never consider all behaviors as a 'natural' part of the growing up process. Parents should have the control over their kids, and not the other way around. Unfortunately, the opposite sometimes becomes even more apparent.

How Kids Use Passive Aggression to Control Parents

When kids ask for space and when you always comply with such demands, you are actually giving them upper hand. Kids get overly frustrated when parents do not listen to them, and experts say that it is OK to respond that way. Once you comply with their every word, you are actually being trained to give up and to eventually leave them alone. The more you do this, the worse the passive aggression gets. Sadly, this is one of the biggest mistakes of overly loving parents.

Passive Aggression also often manifest in the so-called 'learned helplessness', a concept that kids can easily grasp and apply. This idea basically lets kids to appear helpless so they would be excused from doing their chores. Thus, they tend to learn how to resist you and become more passively aggressive if you show them your tougher side.

Many experts also point out that childhood and the adolescence stages are crucial for the children development and learning process. If you are constantly controlled by your kids, you are actually letting them get things their way and will not be able to learn sufficient skills and instill discipline. This will inevitably have a huge impact in their behavior as adults.

The Advantage of Showing Anger Even When Kids are Around

Many may say that expressing anger where kids can witness is can leave them scarred. This is completely false, as children also need to understand that it is natural to express anger and that there is a proper way to show it. The expression of anger is not for kids to be traumatized, but for them to see how anger can turn from conflict to a resolution.

The key is to show your children the right way to angry that involves voicing out your concerns, presenting your arguments, and also listening to the other person. The process by which a problem is resolved by openly discussing it is a good and healthy way to train your kids to become more expressive of their problems.

In general, your kids need to know how to handle anger effectively. Frustrations need to be discussed and issues have to be resolved. Some parents also put in place a rule that does not allow them to go to bed if a conflict remains unsolved. This is another way of instilling the values of open communication and trust: two very important ingredients of maintaining healthy relationships.

If children display other behavioral problems apart from being passive-aggressive, it would be best to have them assessed by a child psychologist. Kids who are unable to express themselves may have other physiological causes that have to be identified. Remember that psychological issues, such as depression and other cognitive-based problems, may be experienced even by very young children.

Quick Guidelines on How to Help Children Become More Expressive and Responsive

There are ways on how you can help your children who have the tendencies to hide their real feelings towards you, the school, or anyone. These tips can also help you address the behavior of children who are being resistant to you.

1. Teach him to keep his bedroom door unlocked or open when he is around. This often lets them understand that you are keeping the barriers to minimum. You can check once in a while when doing their homework. You may offer them help if you can see that they are difficulties completing a task. Tell them that they can call you anytime for difficult homework, too.

2. Reduce distractions such as gadgets or television at home. These components broaden the space between the children and the parents. Allow them to watch television only when homework is done. Try to set rules on the use of the gadgets.

3. No phones during mealtime. Mealtime must be also seen as an opportunity to discuss. As much as possible, try to use a positive tone when asking about their day at school. Start with a question about a topic they are interested in. For example, ask them about the next basketball or soccer game. Never bring up any negative topic during the meal. Problems are better discussed in the bedroom and not in front of the entire family.

4.   Give them a boost. If a certain task or homework is a bit difficult for them to do, try doing the first part. This process is modeling and it helps them see how things are done effectively. Never do the entire work for them. Use this as an opportunity to do things together. Your presence will make them realize that you are willing to help them become a better person.

5.   Never give up. Parents would often surrender when situation becomes extremely difficult to handle. This would resort to blaming the other people in the family. As a parent, you are built to become the pillars of your family. Do not let yourself crumble. Try and try again even if you fail. Your persistence will teach them a lesson in the end.

6.   Explain to the kids the consequences of being inactive and non-responsive. Failing to do a task always has a consequence. Use this principle to explain to the kids why it is important to comply. For example, failing to go to bed early may cause him to miss his field trip or being unable to complete homework may require him to attend additional classes after school.

7.   Set specific time frames. Well, it is sometimes acceptable to give children ample space. However, this should only be allowed   within a specific time frame. Letting them think of their own can give them also a chance to rehearse what they want to say and how they are going to say it. As parents, you need to let them know about this limit. You may say, " Ok, I will give you 30 minutes to think about it, but after that we will talk."

8.   Be careful with the reward system. Giving your kids a boost through rewards is OK and for many parents, this method works. However, you need to remind the children of their responsibilities. And those duties are not always rewarded. Giving too much of a reward can make kids highly dependent on the idea of gaining something for every small did he does. Send the right message when offering rewards.

How Parents Should Encourage Kids to Talk about Anger

This part is quite tricky but holds the key to resolving passive aggression in kids. It is important, however, as being able to encourage your children to speak will teach them to resolve conflicts effectively. Using simple expressions such as, " If you are angry about something that happened today, please know that you can share it with me and we can talk about it. Maybe I will be able to help you with it." Another example is to also emphasize what you expect from the kid. For instance, you may say, " Mommy knows you are angry, but still, I expect you to finish your homework before dinner. After that, we can talk about your problem, I promise."

It is also crucial for children to understand the

consequences and the results expected, regardless how they feel. This will essentially help them speak their thoughts. Moreover, this will also teach them not to make excuses in the future. Accountability is likewise an important aspect to be discussed.

Although this may sound extreme, but there are now training and seminars designed to empower parents. These talks help parents understand the emotional barriers they have with their children. Though some may be pricey, it is never a bad idea to spend a few hundred of bucks if it will improve your relationship with your children. More importantly, these efforts will likewise build them a brighter future.

These training may also help you regain control of your children and of your life as a parent, too. This is an opportunity that will help you understand the importance of being firm. There would be no more walking on extra sensitive eggshells when dealing with your kids. You will also learn to accept that passive aggression is a behavioral problem, and not a psychiatric one. You will also help yourself eliminate power struggles and eliminate the frustration from unceasing arguing with your children.

Overall, the passive-aggressive behavior demonstrated by a child is an ineffective coping mechanism that has to be eradicated. It is your duty as your parent to recognize the behavior and take action against it. You will also have to guide children in developing another coping skill to replace passive aggression.

Parents will always be parents at the end of the day. Whilst it is important to deal with passive aggression, it is also equally important to highlight the positive contributions of the children to your family. You will have to let them understand that regardless of their behavior, they are loved just the same.

Conclusion

If you feel the need to make people react in an angry way by roundabout means such as talking about them with colleagues or creating situations where anger is achieved, then try to steer yourself away from it. You are succumbing to passive aggressive behavior. What this means is that you have self-doubt. Instead of using your normal tactics to overcome these doubts, try to build on what you know to be your positive attributes. For example, someone who can build up the good things about themselves doesn't have to resort to expressing anger through others. Try taking up hobbies that allow you to express yourself in a positive manner. Drama and even singing lessons can really help because they allow the voice to be heard. They may even help in situations when you need to speak publicly. Having your voice heard in an open way is much more satisfactory long term than the short terms kicks you get through playing "mind games."

Although there are many people that you come into contact with during the course of a lifetime, those that you will remember for all the wrong reasons will be those who made you angry inside about circumstances that didn't actually involve "them." The passive aggressive person revels in a celebration when able to pass anger on to someone else. It gives them a sense of power. It fights back all of those thoughts that have been in their mind since childhood about not having a voice that matters sufficiently for anyone to listen to it. The problem is that the negativity spread by people who need to do this can knock people with no self-esteem issues for six because these are the least suspecting of the game being played.

The better way forward for those who prefer to know their true friends is to observe, to listen and learn to avoid confrontation caused by the chattering of others. If you find yourself upset with someone, give yourself space to think things through. Examine whether the anger you are feeling is inappropriate or whether someone has engineered it. Once you recognize the game that passive aggressive people play, you will be able to avoid the sting of being hurt by them. If you think that you have passive aggressive tendencies, it's worthwhile remembering that the problem doesn't come from the people you cause problems to. The problem comes from the way that you perceive your own self-worth. Instead of making others act out your anger, it's far more beneficial to learn to like yourself, to celebrate your worth. Parents make all kinds of mistakes when they are bringing up children. No parent is perfect. Some a very good at the job that they do, and you can see from looking around you at happy people the kind of thing that happens when you get a balanced upbringing.

Use these people as role models. Find your own worth, because the trips laid upon you by your parents may not actually be based on anything short of inexperience on their part. Your father may have been authoritarian in his approach because he learned this from his own father. Your mother may have been submissive in her approach to his will, but that's also something she learned as a child.

The point now is that you have had passive aggressive behavior explained to you and you are now an adult, able to break that vicious circle. Once you do, you become a much more balanced and happy individual that doesn't depend upon the misery of others to make you feel in control. Look at your positive attributes. Work to build your self-esteem and to counter balance all the negativity from your childhood. Chances are that as you do, you will find passive aggressive behavior isn't actually necessary to have an impact on people. The response you get from simply being you will be enough to sustain you and make you happy. That's when you know you have this thing beat!

RECOMMENDED READING!

PSYCHOPATH: Manipulation, Con Men And Relationship Fraud
smarturl.it/psychoa

NARCISSISM: Self Centered Narcissistic Personality Exposed

hyperurl.co/narc

Personality Disorders: Borderline Personality Disorder: Beauty Queen or Emotional Terrorist?

hyperurl.co/emotionalterror

Personality Disorders: Histrionic and Borderline Personality Disorders **Unmasked**
hyperurl.co/borderline

TAKE GOOD CARE OF YOURSELF!

Anger: Natural Treatments To Manage Frustration And Stress

hyperurl.co/anger

SELF ESTEEM: Confidence Building: Overcome Fear, Stress and Anxiety: Self Help Guide

hyperurl.co/selfesteem

HEALING: Heal Your Body Heal Your Life

smarturl.it/healingaa

SUGAR: Shut Your Mouth To Sugar Addiction And Cravings Forever

hyperurl.co/sugar

Made in United States
Orlando, FL
24 October 2022

23784911R00068